D1032885

A Robbie Reader

Tiki Barber

Joanne Mattern

Marysville Public Library
231 South Plum Street
Marysville, Ohio 43040
(937) 642-1876

Mitchell Lane
PUBLISHERS

P.O. Box 196
Hockessin, Delaware 19707
Visit us on the web: www.mitchelllane.com
Comments? email us: mitchelllane@mitchelllane.com

Mitchell Lane PUBLISHERS

Copyright © 2007 by Mitchell Lane Publishers. All rights reserved. No part of this book may be reproduced without written permission from the publisher. Printed and bound in the United States of America.

Printing   1   2   3   4   5   6   7   8   9

A Robbie Reader
Contemporary Biography

Alex Rodriguez	Brittany Murphy	Charles Schulz
Dakota Fanning	Dale Earnhardt Jr.	Donovan McNabb
Dr. Seuss	Hilary Duff	Jamie Lynn Spears
Jesse McCartney	Johnny Gruelle	LeBron James
Mia Hamm	Shaquille O'Neal	The Story of Harley-Davidson
Syd Hoff	**Tiki Barber**	Tony Hawk

Library of Congress Cataloging-in-Publication Data
Mattern, Joanne, 1963–
   Tiki Barber / by Joanne Mattern.
      p. cm. – (Robbie reader)
   Includes bibliographical references and index.
   ISBN 1-58415-522-1 (library bound)
   1. Barber, Tiki, 1975- —Juvenile literature. 2. Football players—United States—
Biography—Juvenile literature. I. Title. II. Series.
GV939.B365 2007
796.332092—dc22
[B]   2006014819

ISBN-10: 1-58415-522-1   ISBN-13: 9781584155225

ABOUT THE AUTHOR: Joanne Mattern is the author of more than 100 nonfiction books for children. Along with biographies, she has written extensively about animals, nature, history, sports, and foreign cultures. She wrote *Brian McBride, Peyton Manning, Miguel Tejada,* and *Dakota Fanning* for Mitchell Lane Publishers. She lives near New York City with her husband and three young daughters.

PHOTO CREDITS: Cover, pp. 18, 21 — Paul Spinelli/Getty Images; p. 4 — Julie Jacobson/AP Photo; p. 6 — Nick Laham/Getty Images; p. 8 — Getty Images; p. 12 — Doug Pensinger/Allsport/Getty Images; p. 14 — Ezra O. Shaw/Allsport/Getty Images; p. 15 — Craig Jones/Allsport/Getty Images; p. 17 — Peter Muhly/AFP/ Getty Images; p. 20 — Jeff Chiu/AP Photo; p. 22 — Paul Schmulbach/Globe Photos; pp. 24, 26 — Scott Eells/Getty Images.

ACKNOWLEDGMENTS: The following story has been thoroughly researched, and to the best of our knowledge represents a true story. While every possible effort has been made to ensure accuracy, the publisher will not assume liability for damages caused by inaccuracies in the data, and makes no warranty on the accuracy of the information contained herein. This story has not been authorized or endorsed by Tiki Barber.

PLB

TABLE OF CONTENTS

Chapter One
Keeping His Promise 5

Chapter Two
Family First 9

Chapter Three
Working Hard in the NFL 13

Chapter Four
Tiki On Top 19

Chapter Five
Helping Others 23

Career Rushing Stats 27
Chronology 28
Find Out More 29
Works Consulted 29
Glossary 31
Index 32

New York Giant Tiki Barber breaks free from Kansas City Chief Kendrell Bell during their game on December 17, 2005. The Giants went on to win the game.

Keeping His Promise

For many years, the New York Giants football team had not been playing very well. They lost more games than they won. In 2005, things changed. They started winning more games.

Tiki Barber was a **running back** for the Giants. He was one of the best players on the team. He and his teammates were happy to have a winning season.

However, there was sad news, too. In 2005, the team's owner, Wellington Mara, was very sick. The Giants knew that Mara would die soon.

When Tiki visited Mara in the hospital, he made a promise to the Giants' owner. He told

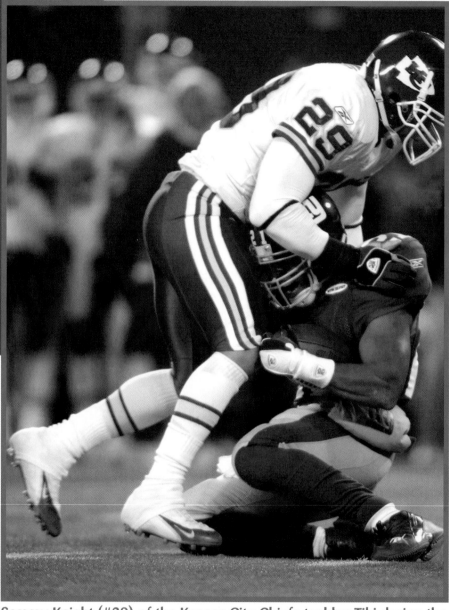

Sammy Knight (#29) of the Kansas City Chiefs tackles Tiki during the December 17, 2005, game. The Chiefs could not stop Tiki from rushing for 220 yards.

Mara that he and the Giants would always do their best.

Mara died on October 25, and Tiki kept his promise. On December 17, the Giants played the Kansas City Chiefs. Tiki **rushed** for 220 yards. This was a new team **record**. The Giants beat the Chiefs 27-17.

"It feels really good," Tiki said after the game. The win had put the Giants one step closer to their goal: to play in the Super Bowl.

The Giants did not make it to the Super Bowl that **season**. However, they knew they were a great team. Tiki Barber knew this too. He had spent his whole life working hard to be the best.

Tiki (#21) and Ronde (#19) Barber walk onto the field with their mother before playing a college game for the University of Virginia.

Family First

Jamael Oronde Barber and Atiim Kiambu Barber were born on April 7, 1975, in Roanoke, Virginia. Jamael was nicknamed Ronde. Atiim was called Tiki. They are **identical** twin brothers. Tiki is seven minutes younger than Ronde.

Their father, James Barber, had played football in college. Their mother, Geraldine Barber, worked as an **administrator** for the Girl Scouts.

Like many twins, the Barber boys were born several weeks early. They were so small and sick, they had to stay in the hospital for a month. Finally, the boys were strong enough to go home.

There was a different kind of trouble at home. James and Geraldine Barber did not get along. When the twins were four years old, their father left. Geraldine raised the boys by herself. "It was all Mom," Ronde said. "Mom was both parents."

Geraldine Barber wanted the best for her young sons. She worked for the Girl Scouts during the day. Then she came home to be with her boys. At night, she had a second job. "It was a struggle for her," Tiki said later.

Tiki and Ronde did everything together. They even got into trouble together. Geraldine remembers times when "both of them got spanked because I didn't know who had done what."

The boys were close to their mother, too. The principal of their junior high once said, "They were such a team as a family."

Sports were very important to Tiki and Ronde. They were on the track team at Cave Spring High School. Tiki was a **sprinter**. Ronde was a champion at the **hurdles**. The twins were stars on the school's football team too.

Doing well in class was even more important than sports. Tiki and Ronde's friend Chris Vaughn said, "After dinner, they'd go straight to their homework." If Chris or their other friends wanted to play, the Barber boys would say, "Sorry."

Tiki also loved to read. He said, "My happiest memories as a child involve reading, not sports." He would even take a book with him when he went out with his friends after school.

All that reading paid off. In 1993, Tiki graduated from high school with terrific grades. Ronde did, too. Then it was time to go to college.

Tiki's teammates congratulate him after the University of Virginia defeats
Duke University in October 1995.

Working Hard in the NFL

Tiki and Ronde chose to go to the University of Virginia. Tiki won a **scholarship** to go—not because he played football, but because of his outstanding grades.

Tiki worked hard in the classroom and on the football field. He set many school records. When he graduated, he had rushed for 3,389 yards on the football field. Only one other player at the University of Virginia had more rushing yards than Tiki. Tiki also set records for the school's track team.

In 1997, Tiki and Ronde graduated from the University of Virginia. Both brothers wanted to play in the National Football League, or NFL.

Tiki was **drafted** by the New York Giants. Ronde was drafted by the Tampa Bay Buccaneers.

Many people thought Tiki would not be a strong player. He was only five feet, ten inches tall and weighed about 200 pounds. That is small for a football player.

Tiki surprised everyone with his football skills. In 2000, the Giants made it to the Super Bowl. Tiki led the team in rushing and receiving

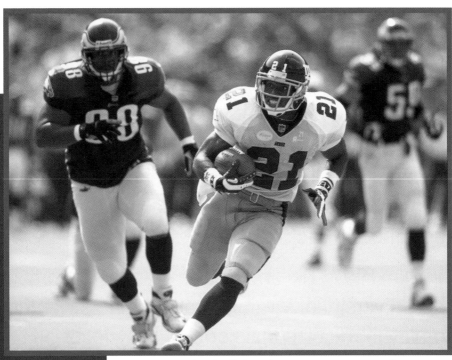

Tiki carries the ball during a game in 2000 between the New York Giants and the Philadelphia Eagles.

Tiki's twin brother, Ronde, runs with the ball during a game against the New York Jets. He plays for the Tampa Bay Buccaneers.

during the Super Bowl game; however, the Giants lost badly. The Baltimore Ravens beat them 34-7.

In 2002, Tiki scored a career-high eleven rushing touchdowns. That was the best record by a Giants player in ten years. That year, Tiki also became the first player since 1970 to make a rushing play of at least 40 yards in four straight games.

15

During Super Bowl XXXV, Rod Woodson of the Baltimore Ravens tries to tackle Tiki. The Ravens went on to defeat the Giants, 34-7.

Tiki had another strong year in 2003. For the fourth straight year, he led the Giants in rushing. He also led the team with 69 receptions.

However, Tiki had a big problem. He **fumbled** the ball a lot. Between 2000 and 2003, he dropped the ball 35 times.

In 2004, Tom Coughlin became the new head coach of the Giants. Coughlin hated fumbles. He told Tiki that his fumbles were hurting the team. Tiki knew he had to do better.

Tiki changed the way he held the football. Instead of holding it away from his body, he stood up straight and held the ball close.

He also began lifting weights. His chest and arms got very strong. This helped him hold on to the ball.

Tiki knew he was a better player now. He would help his team do better, too.

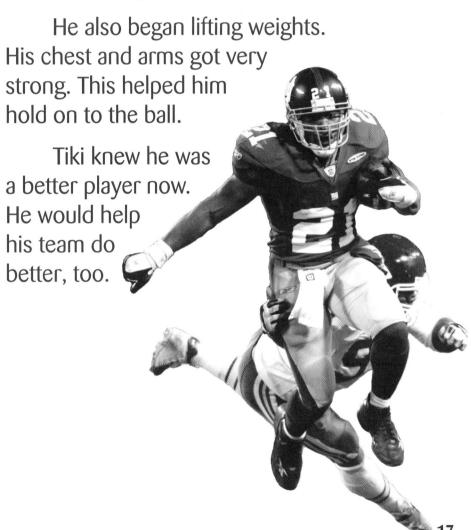

Football can be a rough game! During the 2006 Pro Bowl, Champ Bailey of the Denver Broncos knocks Tiki right off his feet.

Tiki on Top

Tiki worked hard for his team. In 2004, he rushed for 1,518 yards and received for 578 yards for a total gain of 2,096 yards. He also scored 15 touchdowns. He was chosen to play for the **NFC** in the NFL Pro Bowl/All-Star game.

However, the Giants did not have a good year. They lost ten games and won only six.

Tiki was sure the 2005 season would be better. He was right! During that season, Tiki was a team leader. He rushed for more than 200 yards in three different games during 2005. He gained a total of 2,390 yards that season. The Giants ended the season with eleven wins and only five losses.

Tiki was amazing during the last game of the season. He ran 95 yards to score a touchdown and beat the Oakland Raiders. He broke a Giants record for the longest touchdown run. That record had not been broken for 75 years! Tiki was also chosen to play in his second NFL Pro Bowl.

The Giants made it to the NFC Championship. They would play the Carolina

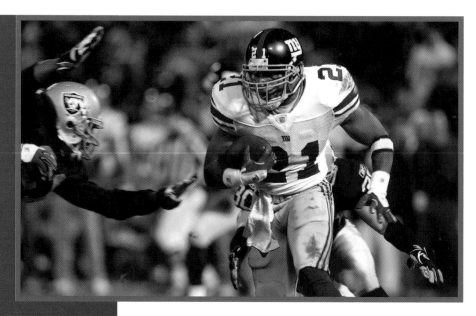

Tiki rushes for a touchdown during a December 31, 2005, game against the Oakland Raiders. He set a team record of 50 rushing touchdowns.

Tiki runs the ball during the 2006 Pro Bowl in Honolulu, Hawaii. The NFC went on to win, 23-17.

Panthers. The winner of that game would go on to play in the Super Bowl.

The Panthers beat the Giants in the NFC Championship. Tiki was upset that the Giants did not win. He said that the team did not play as well as they should have. However, he knew the Giants were still a good team. They would have another chance next year.

Tiki and his wife, Ginny, attend a benefit for the Fresh Air Fund in New York City in June 2006. They go to many charitable events together.

Helping Others

Football is a big part of Tiki Barber's life. However, he has many interests outside the game.

He has a strong family life. Tiki and Ginny Cha met when they were in college. They got married in 1999 and have two sons: AJ, who was born in 2002, and Chason, who was born in 2004. The family lives in New York City.

Tiki remains close to his mother and brother. He and Ronde have written two children's books together. *By My Brother's Side* was published in 2004. *Game Day* was published in 2005. Both books show how the brothers helped each other to do their best.

Tiki holds a young fan at a benefit for the Elizabeth Glaser Pediatric AIDS Foundation in 2004.

Reading is very important to Tiki. He has been a Verizon **Literacy** Champion since 2001. Through this program, he helps children and adults in New York City learn how to read. He and Ronde also took part in a Read Across America campaign held by the National Education Association.

Tiki gives his time and money to help people in other ways. He raises money for the Children's Miracle Network, the Ronald McDonald House, and the Fresh Air Fund. These **charities** all help children and families.

Tiki knows he will not be able to play football forever. He is interested in working in broadcasting. He already appears on the Fox News Channel show *Fox and Friends.* He and Ronde have a show on the radio, too. The show is called *Barbershop.*

Tiki faced a big decision in 2006. Would that be his last season in the NFL? He thought he would like to **retire**. He would like to do more work in broadcasting. However, Tiki would also love to win the Super Bowl. He said

Tiki and Ronde proudly show off their children's book, *By My Brother's Side*, at a book signing in New York City.

that if the Giants won a Super Bowl in 2006, "that would be a sign to walk away. . . . If I had to, I would walk away without one. . . . [But] I want to be where I am now *with* a Super Bowl ring."

Tiki has always worked hard to be the best. "I'm one of the luckiest guys in the world," Tiki says. His strong family life and desire to work hard have made him a huge success, both on and off the field.

CAREER RUSHING STATS

YEAR	TEAM	G	GS	ATT	YARDS	AVG	LG	TD	20+	FD
1997	NYG	12	6	136	511	3.8	42	3	2	31
1998	NYG	16	4	52	166	3.2	23	0	1	8
1999	NYG	16	1	62	258	4.2	30	0	1	12
2000	NYG	16	12	213	1006	4.7	78	8	9	38
2001	NYG	14	9	166	865	5.2	36	4	8	40
2002	NYG	16	15	304	1387	4.6	70	11	12	67
2003	NYG	16	16	278	1216	4.4	27	2	4	66
2004	NYG	16	14	322	1518	4.7	72	13	11	77
2005	NYG	16	16	357	1860	5.2	95	9	16	72

(NYG=New York Giants, G=Games, GS=Games started, Att=Attempts, AVG=Average yards gained per attempt, LG=Longest run from **scrimmage**, TD=Season touchdown total, 20+=20 or more rushing yards from scrimmage, FD=First downs)

1975   Tiki and Ronde Barber are born in Roanoke, Virginia, on April 7.

1979   Their father leaves the family.

1993   Tiki graduates from high school; he starts college at the University of Virginia.

1997   Tiki graduates from the University of Virginia with a degree in commerce. He is drafted by the New York Giants.

1999   Tiki marries Ginny Cha.

2002   Their son AJ is born.

2004   Their son Chason is born. Tiki gains 2,096 yards and scores 15 touchdowns; he plays in the Pro Bowl. Tiki and Ronde's children's book, *By My Brother's Side*, is published.

2005   Tiki achieves a total of 2,390 yards (a club record of 1,860 rushing yards, plus 530 receiving); he sets a team record with a 95-yard touchdown run and leads the Giants to the NFC Championships; he is chosen to play in the Pro Bowl. Tiki and Ronde publish their second children's book, *Game Day*.

2006   Thirty-one-year-old Tiki begins what may be his last season in the NFL.

For Young Readers

Barber, Tiki and Ronde. *By My Brother's Side.* New York: Simon & Schuster Books for Young Readers, 2004.

Barber, Tiki and Ronde. *Game Day.* New York: Simon & Schuster Books for Young Readers, 2005.

Works Consulted

Elliott, Josh, and Kostya Kennedy. "Tiki Barber," *Sports Illustrated,* December 13, 2004, vol. 101, issue 23, p. 35.

Finkel, Jon. "Giant Among Men," *Men's Fitness,* November 2003, vol. 19, issue 11, pp. 62–65.

Harris, Jaime C. "Tiki, the Lil Big Man, Has Giant Records and Super Bowl Dreams," *New York Amsterdam News,* December 22, 2005, vol. 96, issue 52, p. 44.

Judge, Clark. "Tiki Still Carries Torch for Title–But For How Long?" CBS SportsLine.com. http://cbs.sportsline.com/print/nfl/story/9584933/2

Lambert, Pam. "Having a Ball," *People,* January 29, 2001, vol. 55, issue 4, pp. 91–93.

Pedulla, Tom. "Despite Small Stature, Barber Is a Cut Above," *USA Today,* December 21, 2005, p. 4C.

Red, Christian. "Hanging in the Flat with Tiki." *New York Daily News*, January 8, 2006.

Web Addresses

NFL.com—Tiki Barber
http://www.nfl.com/players/playerpage/1782
New York Giants—Player—Tiki Barber #21
http://www.giants.com/team/
  player.asp?player_id=4
SI.com—Tiki Barber Player Page
http://www.cnnsi.com/football/nfl/players/3937
Smith, Katherine. "Barbers Are a Team of Their Own."
http://multimedia.tbo.com/multimedia/popup/
  MGAXZRMFCND.html

administrator (ad-MIH-nih-stray-tur)—A person who runs an office.

charities (CHAA-ruh-teez)—Groups that collect money to help people in need.

drafted (DRAF-tud)—Chosen to play on a team.

fumbled (FUM-buld)—Dropped the football.

hurdles (HER-dulz)—A track event in which a runner jumps over small fences.

identical (eye-DEN-tih-kuhl)—Exactly the same.

literacy (LIH-tuh-ruh-see)—Being able to read and write.

NFC—National Football Conference; one of the divisions in the National Football League.

record (REH-kurd)—Something that is noted in the history books because it is the best.

retire (ruh-TYR)—To give up work.

running back (RUH-ning bak)—In football, a player who runs with the ball and tries to score.

rushed—In football, ran with the ball.

season (SEE-sun)—The part of the year when a sport is played.

scholarship (SKAH-luhr-ship)—Money given to someone to help pay for school.

scrimmage (SKRIH-midj)—The position of the ball at the beginning of a down, or complete play.

sprinter (SPRIN-tur)—A person who runs fast over short distances.

Bailey, Champ 18

Baltimore Ravens 15, 16

Barber, AJ 23

Barber, Atiim Kiambu (Tiki)
  birth of 9
  charitable work 22, 24, 25
  childhood 10–11
  children of 23
  college 8, 12, 13
  family 9, 23
  and fumbles 16–17
  high school 10–11
  in NFL 4, 5, 6, 7, 13–17, 18–21
  size of 14

Barber, Chason 23

Barber, Geraldine (mother) 8, 9, 10

Barber, Jamael Oronde (Ronde) 8, 9, 13, 14, 15, 23, 26, 27

Barber, James (father) 9, 10

Barbershop radio show 25

Bell, Kendrell 4

By My Brother's Side 23, 26

Carolina Panthers 20–21

Cave Spring High School 10

Cha, Ginny 22, 23

Coughlin, Tom 17

Denver Broncos 18

Fox and Friends 25

Game Day 23

Kansas City Chiefs 4, 6, 7

Knight, Sammy 6

Mara, Wellington 5, 7

New York Giants 5, 7, 14, 19–21

NFC Championships 20–21

NFL Pro Bowl/NFC All-Star Game 18, 19, 20, 21

NFL 13, 19, 20

Oakland Raiders 20

Philadelphia Eagles 14

Super Bowl 7, 14–15, 16, 21, 27

Tampa Bay Buccaneers 14, 15

University of Virginia 8, 12, 13

Vaughn, Chris 11

Woodson, Rod 16